The Distance Formula

poems by

Jacqueline Young

Finishing Line Press
Georgetown, Kentucky

The Distance Formula

Copyright © 2019 by Jacqueline Young
ISBN 978-1-63534-870-5 First Edition
All rights reserved under International and Pan-American Copyright Conventions. No part of this book may be reproduced in any manner whatsoever without written permission from the publisher, except in the case of brief quotations embodied in critical articles and reviews.

ACKNOWLEDGMENTS

Many thanks to the following journals in which some of these poems appeared:

Entropy: "Metempsychosis" "You Can Be Here, But Only Right Now" "Ignis Fatuus"
The Rush: "The Bath."
Hobart: "To-may-to To-mah-to" "An Hour or Two of Guided Meditation" "Origins of the Milky Way" "Acquiesce" "The Distance Formula"

Publisher: Leah Maines
Editor: Christen Kincaid
Cover Art: Jacqueline Young and Rebecca Ann Jordan
Author Photo: Pablo Garcia
Cover Design: Leah Huete

Printed in the USA on acid-free paper.
Order online: www.finishinglinepress.com
also available on amazon.com

Author inquiries and mail orders:
Finishing Line Press
P. O. Box 1626
Georgetown, Kentucky 40324
U. S. A.

Table of Contents

Hotel Monte Vista 1
The Bath 2
Cosmographia 3
Quote for the Uninsured 4
Regret 5
Blame 6
Housekeeper 7
Walking Around the House, Cradling / a Bag of Grapes 8
I Watched Him One Morning While He Buzzed Around / Up There, Up Where the Mirror Touches the Ceiling 9
Sofa-stry 10
Ignis Fatuus 11
How to Apologize and Mean It 12
How to Do Things with Words 13
To-may-to To-mah-to 14
Acquiesce 15
An Hour or Two of Guided Meditation 16
Origins of the Milky Way 17
The Distance Formula 18
Don't Worry, It Will Happen So Fast / We Won't Feel a Thing 19
If Only We Were Statues 20
How to Disappear Completely 21
The Memory 22
Basic Meteorological Concepts and Other Phenomena 23
A Brief History of Swimming 24
Contents of the Voyager Golden Record 25
Metempsychosis 26
You Can Be Here, But Only Right Now 27

Hotel Monte Vista

The neon sign burns
somewhere out beyond Barstow

    Vacancy
Like two bare arms stretched

        Humbert Humbert at his desk
        measuring rotation curves for planetary nebulae

The Bath

I float
roll from side to
side, favor
my right

sometimes my nipples
poke holes
in the surface

come up
for air

below: a sea
anemone—its
many thin tentacles wave
back and
forth

when I shave my legs
short hairs
float up

eventually
sink

excrement
of small fish

I slip—

Cosmographia

We spread the hours
in every direction

slid our palms
across its terrain

did time start
here?
we asked

again
the first time

Quote for the Uninsured

As if tying a rope
around our waists

were enough to ensure
our entry would be

the same
as our escape

Regret

To the left of the sternum

a tunnel

approximately
horizontal

at the end of which lies
a vortex of light—

If peered through
with one eye closed

you might be occupied
by the way it seems to move

cyclical
searching itself

Blame

As if any old object
could contain it

the heart a packrat

accumulates—
    loose change, bobby pins

Housekeeper

The cat sleeps on
the arm
of the couch

she wakes up here
and there
to lap water
into her mouth

or pace the rooms
searching for
a window of sunlight

*

Perched at the window
she occupies herself:

wasp fossilized beneath
a layer of paint

*

In this apartment
just the two of them

in one room
out the other

the shutters
an en dash

need dusting

Walking Around the House, Cradling a Bag of Grapes

As if the bulk of them—
      each body

              an apology

I Watched Him One Morning While He Buzzed Around Up There, Up Where the Mirror Touches the Ceiling

The couch
in the hall

cushioned
the weight

of his fall

so that his body
no longer

became
an anomaly for

his wings

Sofa-stry

The point is, the why
hurts
too much

but this couch
is a good mediator

carrying my weight
the body
says things

I am sad
I am sad

and this couch
with its wooly arms
says

shhh

Ignis Fatuus

Nightmares like night
horses: hooves

against my cranium
the sound of an owl

who's th-
ere?

whose
there

How to Apologize and Mean It

1.
Look up synonyms for the word 'apology'
Note the following: gift, reason, whitewash, excuse

2.
Linger over the phrase 'mea culpa'
the way it suggests

cupped palms

an attempt to contain water
or something longer

3.
Remove your coat
fashion it into a bowl
arm over
wooled arm

How to Do Things with Words

What does it do to confess
when all that follows
is more cruelty

as if we didn't have enough
to carry

as if
in the act of confession
we were compelled
to a reworking?

—Better the lie, better
the bottle whose letter remains
untarnished by the sea

To-may-to To-mah-to

You say tomorrow
I say right now

Let's call the whole thing off

Acquiesce

as in child's pose—

the instructor tells us
to spread our knees

make room
for our bellies
to rest

my belly is full
of last night's
excess

the liquor rolls
I roll with it

An Hour or Two of Guided Meditation

The bathroom fan chants
while I

in half-lotus
pluck stubble from

my belly

Origins of the Milky Way

Supine
my breasts

happily
nourish no

one

The Distance Formula

Each body has
its own
unique
rhythm

I'd rather
you
not listen
to mine

Don't Worry, It Will Happen So Fast We Won't Feel a Thing

At night I write

you would say spin
a whirlpool for

the world
to end

If Only We Were Statues

We wouldn't have to focus
on being

so still

How to Disappear Completely

Light filters through
a gap in the curtains

dust floats constant

I hold out my palm
so only half is sun-lit—

what drifts

The Memory

As if I were capable
of culling it from my mind
like a file
from a drawer

as if
I could fool you
into thinking I
was doing just that

Basic Meteorological Concepts and Other Phenomena

As children
we twirled on grass
praised sunlight

our skirts lifted
gave way to knees
then thighs

the sky was God
which asked
for nothing

A Brief History of Swimming

Our feet
moved slow
in figure
eights

our hands
held tight
the red brick edge
of the pool
at the deep end
near the diving board

our heads
dipped infant
beneath
the surface
all at once

If I told you
I expected
competition

not consonance

would you believe?

Contents of the Voyager Golden Record

Last night I dreamt I was floating
alone in the ocean

fished
letting stars fall

Metempsychosis

The coroner bird
with its twelve foot
reach

replaced the pith
with a pine
cone

whispered
you are not yet
deceased

You Can Be Here, But Only Right Now

Early in the year

the northern bobwhite seeks
cover on dry ground

shy thing

plumage settling
into woody plant
closed-scrub, chaparral

I watch it

as it watches me
one eye concerned
with the rippling of my skirt

the way   my feet shift
loosen dirt

Jacqueline Young is a first generation Vietnamese-American poet and essayist from the Mojave Desert in Southern California. She has served as an assistant editor for the literary publication *Black Clock*, a production coordinator for San Francisco's Litquake and was named a finalist for the 2017 Concrete Wolf Poetry Chapbook Award. She received her MFA in Creative Writing and Critical Studies from California Institute of the Arts. Her poetry can be found in *Hobart, Entropy,* and *The Rush.*

www.ingramcontent.com/pod-product-compliance
Lightning Source LLC
LaVergne TN
LVHW041517070426
835507LV00012B/1641